Communication

A Useful Guide To Improving Your Communication In All Aspects Of Your Business, Together With Suggestions On How You Can Speak Up In Meetings

(Expert Strategies For Succeeding In Public Speaking Proven Strategies To Improve Speaking Skills)

Eberhard Haring

TABLE OF CONTENT

Introduction 1

Effective Communication Is An Essential Competency For Success In Both Personal And Professional Spheres 3

Individuals Engaging In Conflict Instigation And Sustenance 17

Comparing Introverts And Extroverts 36

When Children Pose A Barrier To Intimate Relationships 57

Why Is It That You Are Unable To Engage In Communication With Anyone? 72

Social Factors 104

Tell Me In Mimes How I Am Feeling 128

Implementing Assertiveness In Your Circumstances 145

Introduction

Proficient communication abilities serve as a fundamental method that empowers individuals to articulate thoughts effectively, fostering enriched interpersonal and vocational relationships. Having the ability to attentively listen and effectively communicate will prove beneficial in articulating your thoughts during professional settings such as job interviews and business meetings, as well as in your personal interactions.

To achieve success as a communicator, one must possess the skill to attentively listen and effectively convey one's thoughts to individuals in their vicinity. Unfortunately, there is no singular aptitude or technique that can instantaneously metamorphose into an enhanced communicator. Proficient communication calls for a diverse range of abilities that encompass verbal and nonverbal signals, alongside attentive listening.

Effective Communication Is An Essential Competency For Success In Both Personal And Professional Spheres.

Efficient communication is essential in both professional and personal settings as it allows for the effective transference of one's thoughts and emotions into clear and comprehensible messages. Efficient communication enhances one's productivity while mitigating any unintentional consequences that may arise from misinterpretation. Establishing an effective communication protocol facilitates a comprehensive understanding of others' perspectives while bolstering one's capacity to collaborate and thrive within a team environment.

In order to enhance communication efficacy, it is imperative to cultivate a multitude of essential competencies that synergistically interact with each other. Certain abilities are manifested through one's speech and body language, while others are centered on emotional and interpersonal aptitudes.

Overcome Difficulties

Efficient communication streamlines the entire process of interaction. It will become evident that the act of sharing difficulties and seeking support is considerably more convenient.

The act of collectively surmounting challenges enhances preexisting ties and nurtures a cohesive communal spirit. Furthermore, it facilitates the act of reaching out to others for support and fosters the cultivation of empathy.

• OCD is readily apparent

Individuals suffering from Obsessive-Compulsive Disorder exhibit a tendency towards concealing their compulsive behaviors. And without proactive investigation on your part, the knowledge may forever elude you. Seek recurrent behavioral patterns in order to alleviate anxiety caused by persistent intrusive thoughts. They are not quirks. Obsessive-Compulsive Disorder (OCD) is not a condition which exhibits exclusivity based on race, age, or social class. Without explicit disclosure from the individual affected, there is no definitive means of ascertaining the information. The mental disorder will not be discernible through medical examinations performed at the hospital. Despite the presence of increased brain activity in specific regions on brain scans of individuals with OCD, this evidence alone cannot categorically determine the presence or absence of OCD in an individual. Furthermore, it should be noted that Obsessive-Compulsive Disorder is not easily detectable since not all compulsions are externally observable. Some compulsions manifest as psychological, while others entail rapid actions that are less overt than actions such as hand-washing or wall-tapping.

• Their knowledge is lacking

However, belonging to the same classification as psychiatric disorders due to its impact on the cognitive function, individuals with OCD possess an awareness of their compulsive behaviors. That is the reason why the majority of individuals with OCD conceal their condition, which subsequently leads those without OCD to promptly arrive at the misconception that OCD is an infrequent occurrence. It isn\\\'t. They possess a profound understanding of their actions, the underlying motives, and the potential impact which may be perceived by observers. In addition to their undesirable and fixated thoughts, these individuals experience heightened anxiety that impels them to withdraw from social settings and succumb to their compulsions. A considerable number of individuals afflicted with compulsive disorders are aware of the illogical nature of their thoughts and fears. They comprehend that there is genuinely no peril and that failure to tap on the table uniformly, with all fingers on both hands, will not lead to any catastrophic consequences. The recognition of the illogical nature of these behaviors and the apparent sense of powerlessness accompanying them renders OCD profoundly distressing and disheartening. In contrast to individuals diagnosed with OCPD (Obsessive Compulsive Personality Disorder), who firmly believe in the rationality underlying their need for cleanliness and order, those with OCD experience distress due to their compulsions and actively desire cessation of their obsessive thoughts.

Practice saying no

Notwithstanding the adverse effect it had on my emotional well-being, I consistently acquiesced to situations that caused discomfort, thereby squandering invaluable time. In the beginning, I compelled myself to decline and acquired this expression: "Regrettably, I am unable to fulfill the request." I reminded myself: "Tiana, whenever someone presents a request that I am reluctant to fulfill, refrain from overthinking and simply respond with this phrase." The concept bears a resemblance to the adage: "Assume a facade until you achieve success." Therefore, I initially resorted to feigning by responding, "No, I apologize, but I am unable to accede to your request," until I felt sufficiently self-assured to elaborate on the reasons behind my inability. If posed with the question, "For what reason?" I would respond, "I lack the inclination to perform the task," "I have preexisting commitments," or "I must attend to an alternative obligation." If it pertains to professional obligations, it is essential to furnish a valid justification.

Do not hesitate; instead, exhibit directness. Should an explanation be deemed necessary, it is recommended to provide a succinct account.

Preemptively practice the dialogue you would employ ahead of the occurrence of the situation.

The utilization of the scripting assertive technique may provide assistance in this situation. This methodology enables individuals to premeditate their thoughts using a comprehensive strategy that assists in constructing an efficient discourse.

● The event

Convey a precise depiction of your perception of the situation or problem to the other individual. Peter, the current month's production costs have exhibited a 23 percent increase above the usual average.

● Your feelings

Articulate your sentiments and convey your emotions pertaining to the situation in a descriptive manner. This situation causes me considerable frustration, as it seems to suggest a lack of comprehension or acknowledgement regarding the crucial significance of financial controls within our organization.

● Your needs

Clearly communicate your requirements to the other individual, thereby eliminating the need for any speculation on their part. I kindly request your honesty in promptly notifying me should we exceed the allocated budget significantly for any reason.

● The consequences

Outline the favorable consequences that would arise for the other party or the organization upon the successful fulfillment of your request. If you were to undertake this action, it would greatly enhance our ability to achieve our goals and potentially lead to a more favorable year-end bonus outcome.

If it's challenging to say what you want or think, practice typical scenarios you encounter and know what to say when the situation arises again. If you are currently entertaining the notion that it is senseless to mentally revisit scenarios, I must assert that I have engaged in such an activity based on its practical effect of ensuring preparedness and avoiding quandary in unforeseen circumstances, whereby one might be at a loss for words or unable to conduct oneself in a customary manner. Express your thoughts audibly and ascertain their convincing nature. Try not to stammer. Additionally, it could be advantageous to transcribe your thoughts beforehand, thereby allowing you to rehearse using a prepared text.

At the commencement of my journey, I established a objective: 'I must simply express that'. I did not set my ambitions as high as necessary to convey a persuasive and authoritative tone. Rather, my objective was simply to articulate my thoughts audibly.

Maintain your current stance and reiterate as deemed necessary.

This technique in assertiveness enables one to maintain a sense of ease by disregarding manipulative verbal distractions, argumentative provocations, and irrelevant reasoning, while remaining focused on their standpoint. Utilize a composed and repetitive manner, articulate your desired outcome, and maintain a steadfast resolve on the matter at hand. You will discover that there is no necessity to 'elevate your energy' when engaging with others.

Example:

- Allow me to present to you a selection of our services. - I kindly request the opportunity to showcase a range of our services. - I am eager to demonstrate a variety of our services to you. - It would be my pleasure to exhibit a few of our services for your consideration. - If you would oblige, I would be delighted to present to you some of our services.

- I appreciate your offer, but I am not interested.

- I believe this proposition holds significant potential for your organization, as it has the capacity to effectively minimize expenses while concurrently enhancing productivity.

- While that assertion may possess some validity, my current inclination does not align with pursuing such matters.

- I comprehend that you are occupied with numerous responsibilities. - I acknowledge that you have a demanding schedule. - I am aware that you have a lot on your plate. May I be directed to an alternative individual with whom I can engage in conversation?

- I regret to inform you that I am not interested in availing of the services you are offering. I appreciate your consideration, but I must decline. Thank you.

May I request your permission to send you an email with the intention of requesting your considered opinion or feedback?

- Yes.

- Thank you.

- You\\\'re welcome.

Can you perceive the events that have transpired in this situation? You are merely reiterating the identical expression, albeit with minor modifications. You maintain your stance without expending effort on elaborating its rationale.

Individuals Engaging In Conflict Instigation And Sustenance

Within a team, there may exist an individual who frequently employs tension as a means to instigate conflict, thereby challenging any proposed resolutions. In the majority of cases, the challenge lies not with the individual themselves, but rather with the manner in which they approach problem-solving. They have a repetitive pattern that includes

This member exhibits a proclivity for attributing fault to others, particularly fellow co-workers or team leaders, when confronted with failures or mistakes. They refuse to acknowledge their own shortcomings and instead divert attention by highlighting the deficiencies of others, in order to prevent scrutiny of their own faults.

The individual exhibits a tendency towards dichotomous thinking, whereby they perceive their own proposed solution as the sole viable option and demonstrate reluctance to consider alternative suggestions.

Lack of emotional regulation will give rise to heightened emotions such as fear, anger, and a lack of respect towards other members. This individual tends to allow their emotions to go unchecked, frequently resorting to expressing themselves through social media or online platforms. They harbor a sense of disapproval towards their conduct, despite the fact that the circumstances did not call for such a response. On the opposite side of the spectrum lies the scenario where individuals resort to employing emotional manipulation as a means to attain their desired outcomes.

Manifestations of extreme conduct may encompass engaging in physical altercations, disseminating unfounded hearsay about fellow team members, engaging in persistent surveillance, or making derogatory remarks pertaining to their colleagues.

It is conceivable that these individuals encounter challenges in engaging with others, engaging in introspection, and exhibiting a reluctance to adapt. A connection has been established between individuals who initiate conflicts and specific personality disorders, namely, narcissistic, borderline personality, antisocial, and paranoid personality disorders (Eddy, 2019). Although these individuals may exhibit characteristics associated with these disorders, unless they acknowledge their problem, one cannot anticipate any change in their behavior, and the conflict is likely to escalate in their presence.

It is advisable to make an effort to refrain from engaging in a direct confrontation with them. Rather, prioritize the collaboration among all parties moving forward. Frequently, one can anticipate their disruptive behavior and implement preventative measures to circumvent it. Unless the situation is characterized by toxicity or abuse, it is advisable to consider implementing the subsequent recommendations and exercise caution by maintaining distance from the individual.

Show them compassion and courtesy.

Examine the alternatives at your disposal to effectively handle your association with this individual.

Please ensure that your responses are succinct yet informative, and while maintaining a friendly tone, also exhibit firmness.

By exerting authority over the meeting arrangements pertaining to its timing and location, you have the ability to establish the desired conduct.

Dysfunctional Conflict

When the objectives of the team are sufficiently contested to the point where they become unattainable, the dispute is referred to as dysfunctional conflict. In the course of this phase, the ensuing factors would be evident:

There would be a heightened level of tension, thus rendering the team more challenging to manage than necessary. This would result in elevated levels of anxiety, heightened hostility, and increased frustration.

An elevated rate of employee attrition can potentially engender an environment where team members may experience unease due to persistent tension, leading to a higher frequency of departures and consequently giving rise to diminished productivity levels and dampened team morale.

Elevated dissatisfaction—As team morale diminishes, it results in heightened discontent among team members regarding their working conditions, thereby negatively impacting productivity.

Lack of trust can lead to team members harboring suspicions towards both their colleagues and management, resulting in a decreased sense of camaraderie and a potential aversion to collaboration.

Unachieved objectives - in the presence of team conflict, it may result in diversion of the team's focus from the accomplishment of project goals due to the significant time devoted to resolving differences rather than pursuing project outcomes.

As previously indicated, when conflict becomes prominent within the team, it causes a decline in productivity, which can significantly impact the overall functioning of the organization. Not only would this have implications for income, but it would also influence the company's reputation.

The primary and pivotal Energy Instrument

To provide you with an introduction to these Energy Tools, let us proceed with the process of establishing your Grounding Cord. This constitutes the initial phase of the Daily Energy Routine and serves as an indispensable element for achieving triumph in the realm of animal communication. Indeed, in upcoming chapters, I shall make subsequent references to this specific exercise as we delve into the exploration of surmounting commonplace obstacles that impede your progress toward becoming an animal communicator. It is my desire for you to acquire this knowledge promptly, enabling you to commence experiencing the advantages within your own physical and personal well-being.

Commence by assuming a comfortable seated position on a chair, ensuring that your spine is upright, knees are bent at a right angle, and feet are planted firmly on the floor. Place your hands gently on your thighs, ensuring that your palms are oriented in an upward direction. Please shut your eyes and redirect your attention towards the lower region of your torso. Envision the midpoint situated between your pubic bone and tailbone, denoting the diminutive area of tissue known as the perineum. Visualize a downward trajectory of luminous energy extending seamlessly from your body, traversing through the chair on which you are currently seated, and ultimately penetrating the underlying floor.

Continue to follow that beam of light energy as it moves down and away from you through the foundation of the building you are in and into the earth below. Envision its descent, traversing vertically across every stratum of the planet until it ultimately reaches the core of the Earth. Afterward, ensure that you locate or establish a means to secure it in place. Feel free to exhibit both seriousness and levity, according to your preference.

After establishing the anchorage of your grounding cord, redirect your attention back to your physical form. How does it feel? What do you notice? Are you taking deeper breaths? "Are you experiencing a slight increase in tranquility or a sense of heightened relaxation? Simply observe and take note of your observations.

One remarkable outcome of establishing your grounding cord is the deactivation of your Fight or Flight or Freeze instinct within your nervous system. Upon establishing my grounding cord, I invariably observe a deceleration in my speech pace, deepen my breaths, and experience an enhanced sense of safety and security. You have acquired the knowledge of performing the initial step within the comprehensive five-step regimen of my Daily Energy Routine. I kindly request that you make a regular effort to center yourself and remain vigilant for any discernible alterations or developments that you observe in your physical, mental, and emotional state.

Getting Help

The primary concern you will likely encounter pertains to providing assistance to your child who has recently received a diagnosis of SCD. Seek out a speech therapist who possesses expertise in the field of pragmatic language. A therapist will have the capability to offer personalized individual therapy to address your child's specific challenges.

These children can also derive advantages from participating in a social skills group. The collective setting serves to enhance the skills acquired during the individual therapy sessions. These collectives typically convene on a weekly basis, providing youngsters with an opportunity to enhance their social aptitude within a secure ambiance.

Obtaining insurance coverage for the treatment of sickle cell disease (SCD) might prove to be challenging. This can be attributed to the absence of evidence-based treatment options for SCD, which may be a result of the recentness of the diagnosis. Check to see what coverage your insurance provides with regards to speech therapy, then seek out a therapist from the list they provide.

In the professional setting, superiors predominantly exert their influence through their authoritative power, derived from their official positions. Their positions afford them a certain degree of authoritative privilege. In a formal tone: "Genuine authority can be characterized as the ability to convincingly sway and exert influence over individuals within an organizational structure, irrespective of one's designated rank or role." Individuals wielding genuine authority are indiscernible within the confines of an organizational hierarchy. Genuine authority is partially derived from the exhibited competency to employ analytic reasoning abilities in practical situations. The person who can effectively articulate ideas exudes an inherent sense of genuineness. Genuine authority bestows upon you, as a meticulously prepared and eloquent communicator, a distinct edge. Through the meticulous cultivation and refinement of your message, you attain a sense of credibility, thereby enabling you to engage with the profound reservoir of human sentiments in order to sway and exert influence over your audience, ultimately achieving your desired objective.

If feasible, endeavor to narrow the scope of your objective to one or two preferred outcomes. It is possible that you can consolidate several objectives into a singular goal. Please bear in mind that as a speaker, it is your responsibility to guarantee the delivery of a lucid and cohesive message. Attempting to achieve a multitude of objectives may result in the detriment of your message clarity and the potential for audience bewilderment. In order to maximize the audience's knowledge retention, it is advisable to maintain a straightforward objective. Attempt to succinctly articulate the objective in a single declarative statement. Complexity is the least desirable attribute in a presentation. The expression of ideas beyond a single sentence may potentially exceed the capacity for both effective communication from your side and comprehension and retention from your audience.

With the establishment of your objective, you are now poised to commence crafting your message. It is possible that you are contemplating the idea that the message and the objective may be synonymous. No, your objective is to modify behavior, shift perspectives, exert influence and convince. You are endeavoring to exert an influence on individuals in order to promote the practice of conscientious recycling. However, the objective of your communication is to demonstrate the significance of recycling. Your communication will effectively demonstrate the positive impact of recycling on both the environment and financial sustainability. It is necessary to compose the message with the objective of modifying the behavior. Merely declaring that recycling is beneficial may or may not induce a change in behavior. You would be entrusting the outcome of your presentation to uncertainty. On the contrary, during the course of your speech, it is imperative to persuade your audience about the virtues of recycling, highlight the significance of our collective responsibility towards environmental preservation, and expound upon related notions. Can you discern the discrepancy?

Is it requisite for a presentation to possess a central message? In affirmation, why would one take the effort to assemble it if not? Fundamentally, a presentation entails the collection, structuring, and delivery of information to the intended recipients. It is imperative that the information being conveyed is readily comprehensible to the audience. It is imperative that the audience comprehends precisely the action(s) you desire them to undertake. Draw inspiration from a television commercial. By the conclusion of the brief 30-60 second advertisement, you have gained a precise understanding of the advertiser's intended course of action. The objective of the individual is to persuade you into making a purchase. The underlying message potentially conveys that the utilization of this product or service is likely to augment, elevate, or facilitate the overall quality of your life. It is incumbent upon you to achieve the identical objective with your audience. Your correspondence effectively expresses the enhanced quality of life experienced by individuals upon accomplishing your proposed objective.

Is it possible for there to be multiple messages? Certainly, however, I would advise against excessive transmission of messages to your audience. If an excess of points is made, there is a likelihood that one's audience will struggle to recollect them. A well-constructed message should align with the commonly referred to concept of an "elevator speech." The elevator presentation is a succinct articulation employed when one finds themselves in a brief encounter with their superior, who inquires about their viewpoint on a particular matter. Certainly, you are allocated a duration of less than one minute to express your thoughts. That implies the necessity of focusing exclusively on the central idea and disregarding all other aspects. This is the manner in which the message ought to be unveiled in your discourse. It is the singular aspect that you aspire to etch indelibly in their memory, the unparalleled determinant in the entirety of the presentation.

Comparing Introverts And Extroverts

There exist two distinct personality types: extroverted and introverted. From the preceding introduction, it can be inferred that individuals possessing extroverted traits tend to exhibit higher levels of sociability and demonstrate a propensity for engaging in activities that involve cooperative endeavors, public speaking, or collaborative efforts. Conversely, introverts prefer to independently navigate their surroundings while maintaining a reserved and tranquil demeanor. While extroverted individuals tend to be more proactive, introverted individuals often display shyness, particularly when observed from the perspective of an extroverted manager. I aim to present a fundamental understanding of both concepts.

Extroverts:

Consider extroverts as individuals who excel in social interaction. They thrive in the presence of others, reaching their peak when surrounded by people. For these individuals, a warm evening is characterized by the presence of a few companions gathered around a flickering bonfire; their affection for the company of others is mutual. Their profound display of empathy and their penchant for captivating audiences often leads to an immediate endearment from the majority.

Extroverts manifest characteristics such as warmth, vitality, a keen sense of humor, and an abundance of vitality. However, they are also known to possess high expectations and may exhibit a decline in their productivity if the task they are assigned requires reduced level of focus. Primarily, managers display astuteness by assigning extroverts roles that entail substantial public interaction. As a result, extroverts effortlessly persuade individuals and foster a sense of security, thereby paving the way for enhanced business relationships and heightened profitability. Present an extrovert with an assembly, and by the event's conclusion, he or she will have cultivated favorable relationships with nearly the entire audience.

However, extroverted individuals tend to become easily bored when the focus shifts, disinterested in repetitive tasks, and display shorter attention spans relative to introverted counterparts. Nevertheless, in today's era, effective marketing plays a pivotal role in achieving success across all industries. Consequently, corporate decision-makers are actively seeking to recruit managers who possess extroverted qualities over their introverted counterparts.

Furthermore, individuals who possess extroverted qualities tend to exhibit a willingness to openly express their thoughts and feelings, often without fully considering the potential ramifications. Instances encompass, "Darling, do you believe it would be advantageous for us to relocate to California?"; this by no means indicates a definitive decision, but rather a preference to thoroughly express thoughts, allowing for a clear conscience. Finally, individuals with extroverted personality traits exhibit a broad-ranging network of social connections and invest significant effort into maintaining and nurturing relationships on the outer edges of their network, akin to exemplary marketing strategies.

Introverts

Introverts display a discerning nature, preferring a select few individuals in their company and carefully managing their social interactions as needed. For instance, if an introvert's in-laws visit unexpectedly and, despite having the availability to entertain them, the introvert may express dissatisfaction.

Introverted individuals prefer to maintain a sense of privacy and tend to be more reserved in seeking external attention, particularly until they have become familiar with the group. They possess the ability to effectively pass their time in a bar, primarily engaging in active listening rather than actively vocalizing their thoughts. However, it should not be misconstrued that their limited participation indicates an inability to enjoy themselves. They are afforded the opportunity to derive personal satisfaction, yet in the context of a professional setting such as the workplace, their reticence can frequently result in the allocation of covert tasks.

The reticence exhibited by these individuals primarily stems from apprehension regarding potential mishaps during social interactions, a sentiment that may have originated in their early years. The conduct of an introvert is frequently characterized by timidity, and they appear to place little importance on this attribute within themselves. Please refrain from assuming that shyness is exclusively limited to introverts; extroverts can also experience shyness. However, it is worth noting that extroverts typically exhibit a tendency to eventually overcome their shyness at some stage of their lives. Regrettably, introverted individuals are often perceived as possessing a guarded exterior and exhibiting reluctance to disclose personal information.

Typically, introverted individuals tend to direct their attention towards personal experiences, exhibiting relatively lesser interest in external happenings. The partner of an introverted individual may inquire, "How do you manage to remain composed and engrossed in a film despite the excessive noise being generated by our neighbors?" Introverts possess a remarkable ability to isolate themselves, focusing intensely on their own thoughts and find contentment in their mental state. Are you aware that it is entirely viable for an introverted individual to experience feelings of isolation within a space containing numerous individuals? To those individuals, devoting attention to the lives of others may appear daunting, yet directing their focus towards their own interests, no matter how unexciting it may appear, is deemed the ideal pursuit. They have a propensity for engaging in individual pursuits as opposed to partaking in collective sports.

Likewise, individuals who prefer solitude find it challenging to cultivate personal connections and tend to maintain a succinct social network. They exercise restraint in expressing their thoughts until they have thoroughly deliberated upon them and refrain from discussing matters in which they lack absolute certainty.

5 - Strategies for Crafting Compelling Copy

Recall those illustrations in the Peanuts cartoons, where Snoopy vigorously taps on his antiquated typewriter, situated precariously atop his canine abode, during a night characterized by its dimness and tempestuousness. "A shot rang out. The maid screamed."

We find amusement in the caricature due to its exceptional quality. Poor writing is widespread, not just within the realm of mystery narratives, but also within the domain of nonprofit communications.

As previously stated in the preceding section, effective copywriting commences with a discernible sense of intention, encompassing a comprehensive comprehension of the underlying concept employed, as well as the desired response you aim to evoke from your reader. However, this merely marks the initiation.

If one is unable to articulate their proposition in a persuasive manner, their prospects of success are greatly diminished. The potential recipient of your message may not have the opportunity to access the offer due to the presence of certain obstacles, often referred to as the Bonk Factor. If Chapter Three has not already been reviewed, please consider revisiting it. Therefore, it is of utmost importance to acquire the knowledge and skills necessary for crafting compelling copy. By this, I am referring to writing text that captivates the reader's attention from the very beginning and holds it steadfastly throughout. Similar to an impactful literary work, it captivates the reader, engrossing their senses and imagination through vivid depictions, deep sentiment, and convincing justifications. Am I insinuating to embellish it? Absolutely not. However, if you are unable to effectively convey a level of enthusiasm in your interactions that is capable of convincing others to experience the same emotions as you and subsequently prompt them to act upon those emotions, then you find yourself in a precarious situation.

The Key to Effective Communication with Partners...

There exists a notable disparity between reporting and highly influential, communication strategies that prioritize the needs of donors. Differentiating is straightforward; one can simply examine any appeal or newsletter from the majority of nonprofit organizations. What are the common characteristics exhibited by the majority of direct mail letters or newsletters sent by nonprofits to their mailing lists? Project Updates, Staff Information, Special Needs, Field

Reports, and Perspectives from the Executive Director.

It's a time-honored formula. However, this type of content fails to possess substantial efficacy in cultivating substantial, enduring connections. Why? Due to the ever-changing nature of human relationships, encompassing both moments of exhilaration and despair, periods of uncertainty and resolution, happiness and sorrow, as well as endurance and accomplishment. When you provide your partners with a consistent stream of information devoid of personal engagement—without addressing their interests, concerns, curiosity, desires, and so forth. Failure to do so may result in a reduction of their engagement. It is recommended to adapt your communications in order to prevent the occurrence of the "bonk factor." Familiar with the concept of the "bonk factor?" It refers to the audible impact created when partners involuntarily make contact with the table due to drowsiness caused by repetitive and unengaging information from their field counterparts.

The fundamental principle of communication centered on partners is quite straightforward:

Allocate a greater amount of time and resources towards catering to the needs and priorities of your partners, while diminishing the emphasis on fulfilling your own needs and priorities.

Why is prioritizing this aspect crucial in donor communications? As by providing them with an engaging donor experience, their loyalty will remain unwavering. Crafting well-written content that effectively engages the donor by involving them in the narrative is an integral aspect of that overall experience. It is essential to transcend the conventional approach of merely establishing a connection between the donor and the organization's requirement for their contribution.

Presented herewith are a few illustrations of direct mail copy pertaining to the first page for your discernment... Which option do you believe is more effective and can you explain the reasoning behind your choice?

. Don't Be Stiff

Charismatic individuals possess a remarkable ability to effectively convey their emotions through subtle body language, while still maintaining a balanced and restrained approach. They do not remain stationary and rigid with their arms firmly positioned at their sides while engaged in a conversation. Such behavior is characteristic of individuals who are feeling unease, and it is advisable for you to strive to steer clear of it. A suitable approach would involve maintaining a calm demeanor during a conversation and utilizing appropriate gestures to convey enthusiasm, without exceeding the bounds of moderation. When engaging in the practice of small talk in front of a mirror, observe and take note of the manner in which you utilize gestures. Is your excessive nodding indicative of agreement? Are your hands displaying excessive levels of movement? Although these small gestures may appear insignificant to you, they may be interpreted in varying ways by different individuals. Certain individuals might exhibit a distaste or aversion towards it, while others may experience a degree of unease or discomfort in your presence. Once you have engaged in personal practice sessions before a mirror a few times, seek external evaluations from friends regarding your manner of communication. Are you excessively engaging in a particular activity? Are you failing to fulfill the necessary requirements? Make an effort to seek diverse viewpoints and candid evaluations. This will enable you to discern areas for improvement and recognize your existing strengths. Additionally, it proves beneficial to observe video recordings featuring motivational speakers and presentations delivered by accomplished individuals, in order to grasp their strategies and endeavor to emulate them.

4. Be Witty

One of the exemplary qualities of a person with charisma lies in their ability to effortlessly elicit laughter from others while maintaining an appearance of naturalness. The comedic elements seamlessly intertwine within the conversation, complementing the charismatic individual's effortless demeanor and effortless mannerisms. People have a fondness for individuals who possess the ability to evoke laughter. In order to enhance one's charisma, it is imperative to cultivate the ability to effortlessly elicit laughter in others; that, indeed, is the crux of the matter. The acquisition of charm and the cultivation of a sense of humor can be achieved through the initial step of mastering the art of self-deprecating humor. Demonstrating such capability conveys to others that you possess a sense of self-assurance and ease, displaying indifference towards the possibility of others joining in and sharing laughter alongside you. The initial step entails the ability to embrace self-derision without experiencing any lingering unease. Subsequently, you can acquire the skill of aligning yourself with the comedic sensibilities of others, a task that typically ensues only after engaging in multiple conversations with them. Assess your audience to discern the kind of jokes that are deemed appropriate. As an illustration, in the event that you find yourself in the company of individuals who exhibit a greater degree of sensitivity or discretion, it would be advisable to initially adopt an observant approach and refrain from engaging in humor, so as to avoid the possibility of causing offense. Avoid exerting excessive effort to be humorous due to the pressure of eliciting laughter on every occasion. Select the appropriate occasions and seize the moment when the opportunity arises.

5. Effort to Induce a Sense of Esteem in the Individual You are Engaged in Conversation With

Mastering casual conversation entails possessing exceptional conversational skills that enable you to make your interlocutors feel esteemed, appreciated, and that their viewpoints and thoughts hold significance. It is, in fact, fairly straightforward to accomplish; one must simply commence by exhibiting respect. It is imperative to accord equal treatment to all individuals, devoid of any sense of superiority or inferiority. Demonstrate courtesy towards each individual with whom you engage in conversation, and manifest genuine attentiveness and enthusiasm towards their thoughts and opinions. Inquire in a manner that encourages them to express their perspectives or divulge their insights regarding particular topics. Demonstrate active listening by attentively observing the speaker and responding appropriately, such as by nodding in agreement and offering concise affirmations to convey your engaged participation. Concise interjections may include phrases such as "I understand," or "I concur with that, contingent upon the trajectory of our discussion."

Lastly, it is important to bear in mind that there exists a distinction between being an individual of charm and being a person who strives to constantly appease others. You aspire to be amiable and charismatic, but you are uninterested in becoming overly compliant to accommodate everyone's desires. Individuals who possess charisma exude self-assurance and effortlessly attract others due to the compelling nature of their personalities. If an individual harbors any aversion towards you, it is acceptable considering the inevitable reality that harmony among all individuals is unattainable in this world.

When Children Pose A Barrier To Intimate Relationships

Upon reaching a certain point in one's marital journey and after parenthood has been embraced, it becomes increasingly evident that the offspring one has brought into existence have an enduring and profound impact on the dynamics of romantic affection. They might unintentionally intrude into your bedroom at the exact moment when your partner is engaging in an intimate encounter. Their needs take precedence over your own. As a parent, it is incumbent upon you to prioritize the needs of your children and attend to them promptly. Nevertheless, this should never come at the cost of jeopardizing your relationship. If you observe that the presence of children is significantly impacting your relationship, it is attributed to the insufficient implementation of appropriate strategies.

It is possible that one of you assumes a greater share of domestic responsibilities than the other. It is conceivable that the distribution of jobs has become concentrated in the hands of a single individual, rather than being collectively shared. Sally and Doug were blessed with a pair of offspring. Having children had always been their desire, thus it was never a matter of contention for them. The issue resided in their failure to comprehend the substantial influence children would have on their otherwise exceptional romantic relationship. Sally was required to partake in the nightly procedure of nourishing the infants when they were in their infancy and commenced slumbering whilst partially attired. It was a prudent and logical approach to a predicament that numerous couples must confront. Sally's spouse, Doug, comprehended the infants' requirements and initially scarcely discerned any distinction because, in addition to Sally being awakened, he too frequently experienced disturbance and was obligated to attend work the following day. Subsequently, on a certain day while reclining in bed, he came to the realization that it had been more than a full year since he had last beheld his wife's physique in its unveiled state. That troubled him. When he broached the topic with her, it was done so in a casual manner, without further consideration. Nevertheless, Doug regarded the issue as significant and escalating progressively as long as he refrained from tackling it. He yearned to be reunited with his wife and embrace her affectionately, yet due to her altered sleeping patterns, she rebuffed his advances, exacerbating the issue.

Over time, the couple's communication gradually deteriorated, leading to an instance where Doug returned from work to discover his wife in tears within the confines of their bedroom. He had difficulty comprehending the issue. Her query was whether he perceived her as unattractive following the birth of their children. Naturally, he had not even considered such a possibility; however, she abruptly comprehended that she was dedicating her days to the company of these children. Moreover, when her husband returned home in the evening, the tender intimacy they once shared was notably absent. It was an opportune moment to engage in a constructive conversation. He expressed his exasperation in attempting to approach her and conveyed to her the extent of her beauty and his yearning for their intimate closeness, reminiscent of times past. The infants had undergone such a profound transformation in their way of living that it led to a sense of estrangement for both individuals. She surmised that his lack of initiating sexual activity was due to perceiving herself as unattractive. He ceased to initiate sexual intimacy due to the frequent rejections he encountered when the newborns required feeding every few hours. Both individuals had formed an understanding of each other's emotions, yet both had completely misconstrued the truth.

She perceived that he harbored no interest in her.

● He surmised that she harbored no desire for him.

After surmounting their emotional distress, they reached the conclusion that it was imperative to make alterations in order for them to have dedicated quality time during hours of peak viewership. This would allow them to engage in activities suited for adults without any sense of remorse, affording them the ability to exclude their children from their intimate quarters. They also devised a method by which she could engage in the activities of her choosing, while simultaneously providing her with a modest allowance to purchase personal items. Frequently, women tend to prioritize purchasing items for their babies over attending to their own needs, and she had indeed exhibited this behavior. One day, she meticulously searched through her wardrobe in pursuit of an exquisite garment to wear for Doug's arrival from work. However, she found herself confronted with the harsh reality that her current size had rendered her collection devoid of any alluring options, leading to a well of tears.

Having children does not imply a deprivation of personal time. It is imperative that you adhere to this matter. If you have access to occasional babysitting assistance, then grant yourself a small respite. Having the assurance that the children are in the care of their grandmother facilitates the opportunity for some unguarded adult time, wherein you can partake in shared meals, attend cultural events, and return home to engage in intimate pursuits as desired. The gentle sound of small footsteps should not hinder your romantic pursuits. If both parties seek to express their ardor, it is imperative to devise a mutually agreeable method. If that entails engaging in intimate activity downstairs in the presence of the television, after the children have retired for the night, then that is acceptable as well. Why not? It's your home. The decision ultimately lies within your family, and it is yours to make.

It serves as a source of inspiration for both yourself and those around you.

Engaging in casual conversation has the potential to lead to a remarkable dialogue that can greatly enhance your everyday life and potentially have a lasting, profound impact. In December 2014, my spouse and I attended a Christmas party during which we engaged in conversation with a businessperson following a Minimalist approach, employing light conversation. The entrepreneur was engaged in a business partnership with the employer of my wife.

His discourse delineated principles for embracing a minimalist lifestyle and effectively eliminating superfluous possessions that detract from our life's purpose. Additionally, he imparted to us the notion that prioritizing significant aspects such as nurturing familial bonds and reducing our attachment to material possessions can facilitate personal growth, advance our professional endeavors, and expedite the achievement of our life's aspirations. My spouse and I found it highly motivating, leading us to make a collective resolution for the upcoming year to declutter our possessions in our household. Through the act of philanthropically gifting these items to acquaintances and individuals in need, who would derive value from possessions that no longer serve a purpose in our own lives. Furthermore, it has the added benefit of reducing our daily expenditures, resulting in substantial savings in our bank account within a mere month.

By positioning yourself as receptive to new exchanges and casual conversation, you may ultimately provide assistance to individuals who may not have explicitly expressed their need for help. I recall the encounter I had with another taxi driver while being a passenger in his vehicle, wherein, after engaging in a brief conversation for a duration of three minutes, he started to confide in me regarding his troubles and familial challenges. We engaged in discourse on the subject until I arrived at my destination, subsequent to which I never had the opportunity to cross paths with him again. I am cognizant of the sense of contentment that arose from my ability to offer heartfelt compassion and words of encouragement, which, when he departed, provided relief from his pain. It was gratifying to observe this occurrence. An encounter with individuals who perceive themselves as lacking options for communication has the potential to greatly impact their lives, facilitating the release of repressed emotions and aiding in the organization of intricate thoughts by engaging in articulate dialogue.

It\\\'s unavoidable

The ability to engage in small talk is essential in various professional and social settings such as job interviews, conversing with colleagues, finalizing business agreements, and hosting gatherings with loved ones. In order to integrate within a community, it is necessary to participate in casual conversation. In order to thrive as a prosperous entrepreneur, a capable guide, and a highly proficient staff member, engaging in casual conversation is an indispensable skill. Casual conversation is regarded as a formidable tool in any situation in our lives.

Request guidance

Seek guidance from a more unconventional source when initiating a conversation. It is advised to ensure that the advice sought is of a professional nature and pertaining to your specific situation. Consider this illustration: I am unsure of the appropriate design that should be employed for my show. Do you envision any hindrances to conducting an inquiry and providing me with assistance?

Make an observation concerning a customary behavior.

An alternative approach is to acknowledge a shared action or interest, presuming it is obvious. As an illustration, it is possible to encounter an individual adorned with a badge representing their favorite television program, or observe someone immersed in reading a cherished book while traversing the corridors of your architectural complex. Consider the following scenario: I observed your comprehension of the situation upon our departure from the tram. I recently concluded my reading of that book a week ago. I am curious to know whether you truly hold it in high regard or not.

Make a wisecrack

An alternative approach for initiating a conversation with an unfamiliar individual would be to employ humor by crafting a witty remark. It is most appropriate to do so, provided that the joke is relevant to the situation in which you find yourself with the unfamiliar individual. For instance, have you considered what could potentially diminish the desirability of your Friday? Bearing in mind that it is merely Thursday.

Adapt to the difficulties encountered during the exchange of opinions

Insufficient proficiency in interactive skills may impede one's capacity to effectively participate in conversations, particularly if it conveys an air of hostility. As an example, concrete data suggests that individuals who have social anxiety often uphold consistent eye contact throughout conversations. Nurturing the practice of maintaining visual contact with others during conversations will assist in projecting an aura that is inviting and congenial. This will increase the probability of individuals' receptiveness to your endeavours to initiate a conversation. If one perceives a deficiency in their interactive abilities and the requisite experience to become an adept communicator, availing oneself of self-improvement materials and seeking guidance from a skilled professional can facilitate the enhancement of such skills.

Why Is It That You Are Unable To Engage In Communication With Anyone?

Numerous individuals may experience such a sensation upon their encounter with an entirely unfamiliar environment. The inclination to establish a favorable initial impression when interacting with unfamiliar individuals, coupled with apprehensions of potential rejection due to an inadvertent error, thus shape one's behaviors.

Certain individuals may have had distressing life occurrences wherein they were subjected to instances of neglect, bullying, or social exclusion. Additionally, individuals who possess introverted tendencies encounter this matter as a consequence of their inherent disposition. I would like to draw attention to two distinct groups of introverts in this context.

a) Introverts who exhibit restraint and reserve

b) Individuals who exhibit introverted tendencies and suffer from anxiety.

The aforementioned individuals necessitate a period of acquainting themselves with others. They are unlikely to encounter any difficulties once a specific duration has passed.

With your permission, I would like to suggest that the b) types endure significant distress such as immense embarrassment or fear, rendering them highly likely to be the focus of your inquiry. In light of this advantageous situation, which may require the involvement of others, it is advisable for you to consider seeking professional counseling and formulating systematic remedies. Furthermore, there exists another type of individuals, known as social-introverts, who can also be considered part of this group. However, due to their distinct characteristic of experiencing a depletion of emotional and mental energy when engaging with others, I am of the opinion that they will be equally suited to both situations. These individuals might be mistakenly perceived as introverted, however, they do maintain a select group of acquaintances with whom they cultivate positive social connections.

Cognitive introverts: They may be categorized as individuals with intellectual inclinations or high levels of cerebral engagement. They may be individuals possessing a propensity for profound analysis, opting to maintain a silence during the evaluation of circumstances, individuals, and their interplays. They might be entirely absorbed in an imaginative idea or a fictional reality of their own. It is plausible that individuals may choose to adopt a facade when a critical matter is involved; however, it could prove burdensome to sustain this pretense over an extended duration. Individuals who exhibit traits of social introversion are equally encompassed within this classification.

Individuals who, irrespective of their predisposition as introverts, extroverts, or ambiverts, have developed a cynical perspective due to traumatic experiences, can also experience this issue. For those individuals, the initial step would involve actively facing their fears, coupled with a subsequent recognition of the circumstances in which they must engage with others in order to achieve their personal objectives.

She engages in conversation with you

Should she express interest, it is possible that she will initiate the conversation. Although the initial conversation may have been casual in nature, such as inquiring about your coffee or engaging in small talk, it is evident that she sought a response from you because she initiated the conversation. Think about it. There are individuals present in close proximity, and she engaged in conversation with you. That's awesome!

Alternatively, she may exhibit a similar level of assertiveness as the previously mentioned individual who demonstrated a peculiar attraction towards my name. There are certain women who may not exhibit patience in anticipating your approach, thus it is crucial for you to remain prepared.

So, don't freeze. Please refrain from making any inappropriate or unsettling comments, and instead, politely smile and respond to her. Be casual and nice. Attempt to progress the subject matter in an engaging and playful manner, while refraining from delving into intricate philosophical discourse. Following a brief exchange, it is advisable to acquaint yourself, in the event that you have not yet done so.

What are the indicators to steer clear of?

Sarcasm

There exists a distinction between sarcasm and teasing, nevertheless, discerning between the two can occasionally prove challenging. If one engages in conversation with a woman and finds that her words possess an acerbic quality, occasionally leaving a stinging effect, it is not indicative of one's sensitivity.

It would be advisable to reconsider engaging in this interaction, as should she reciprocate the flirtation, it is highly likely that the outcome will be a challenging experience devoid of any satisfactory conclusion.

The Money Honey

They were previously referred to as individuals engaging in opportunistic relationships for financial gain, but their characteristics are widely recognized. Her sole interest lies exclusively in your automobile, your attire, and your financial assets. She will anticipate you covering her expenses at the bar, including treating her friends to drinks.

While she may respond with laughter to all jests, flutter her eyelashes, and exhibit a captivating smile, it is highly likely that she intends to extract a significant amount of money from you, without granting the privilege of acquiring her contact information. In the event that she accompanies you, it is important to note that she will have certain expectations of being treated with utmost respect and dignity, although it is not guaranteed that she would reciprocate with a kiss.

Occasionally, I refer to these women as "plastic" on account of their artificial smiles, cosmetic enhancements, and conspicuous display of superficial attire adorned with renowned brand logos, all done intentionally to draw attention. Furthermore, I find their dispositions and overall demeanor to be insincere, reinforcing the appellation of "plastic."

The Crazy One

I believe this expression is used excessively, although I must confess my own culpability. The psycho, the crazy. Frequently, it is employed as a designation for a particular action they performed, yet there exist women who justifiably merit the honorific.

Exercise caution when encountering individuals who form attachments hastily and express peculiar remarks under the guise of humor. If they begin to narrate accounts of their involvement in unintentionally causing a fire that resulted in the destruction of their former partner's residence, then it may be prudent to mitigate potential risks and tactfully disengage from the situation.

The Drunk

In my past employment, I was engaged at a widely frequented college bar where it was a recurring occurrence whereby an inebriated female patron would approach me and engage in flirtatious behavior, to which I would reciprocate in a flirtatious manner. Notwithstanding my employment circumstances, it must be acknowledged that engaging in flirtation constituted a component of my professional responsibilities. I would frequently receive invitations to join them at their residence for a beverage following the conclusion of our work, or to participate in social gatherings at bars or parties outside of regular business hours.

I will refrain from making any advances towards a woman who has consumed alcohol while I have not partaken in the same. I would regularly exchange contact information and arrange for social engagements over coffee or dinner during periods when both parties were in a sober state. Allow me to inform you that the aforementioned occurrence significantly fostered a sense of trust when we eventually convened.

Exercise caution around the inebriated young woman. While you may perceive a sense of advancement, it is crucial to acknowledge that her comprehension of your message is deficient, and it is probable that one of her acquaintances will intervene to retrieve her and divert her attention elsewhere. Above all, it is highly likely that she will return home, become unconscious, and have limited recollection of your interaction.

Prior to the situation exacerbating, it is important to note that the seemingly limitless inquiries actually serve a purpose. Their presence serves to notify you of a potential issue before it escalates beyond the point of salvageability. This small reminder serves to mitigate the likelihood of harm befalling something of great worth and significance.

Just as a decelerating car engine complicates everyday life, communication anxiety similarly disrupts your relationship. Indeed, you shall traverse the traffic signal and persist in your journey on a consistent basis, constantly reaffirming the notion of flawlessness owing to the apparent functionality of your automobile's engine. However, there will inevitably be an occasion where the complete capabilities of your engine become indispensable, leading you to question the root cause for its malfunction.

Therefore, what is your approach to addressing these inquiries in a manner that minimizes the likelihood of unintentionally precipitating the very outcome we are concerned about?

Some practical suggestions to facilitate the process

Initially, it should be noted that no legal statute obligates you to promptly address and engage in dialogue regarding the aforementioned issue. Consequently, take your time. There is no urgency to hasten. Efficiently addressing challenges is more favorable than handling them without energy or determination.

Furthermore, it is imperative to resist succumbing to anxiety. Through this exertion, you will have the authority to govern your emotions, rather than being subjected to their whims.

It would be highly advantageous to devote sufficient time to addressing the matter in this particular instance. The apprehension shall diminish with the passage of time. Upon careful contemplation, individuals are inclined to approach the subject matter with reduced affectivity (e.g., frustration, panic, anxiety, etc.), thereby enhancing the likelihood of achieving favorable outcomes. During periods when one or more parties exhibit heightened emotional intensity, engaging in discussions becomes markedly challenging.

Ultimately, it is imperative to address the issue (conduct) rather than fixate on the individual involved (your significant other). We desire that our partner(s) comprehend that the behavior is bothersome, yet it is not directed towards their personal character. Ensure that you introspect and adequately consider your approach, demonstrating appropriate verbal communication. Alternatively, the apprehension would experience further escalation. If your partner possesses strong principles, they will be capable of handling the matter with increased efficiency, ultimately demonstrating through constructive communication that there is no cause for apprehension.

Comprehend the origins of your apprehension.

In perilous surroundings, the instinct of fear conservation proves to be advantageous. Nevertheless, with regards to apprehensions related to communication, the circumstances do not pose a significant threat. Communication anxiety is further elicited by the apprehension of being subject to judgment by the individual one intends to engage in conversation with. Gaining insight into the legitimacy of your anxiety will enable you to effectively manage and address it.

As an illustration, suppose you have recently entered into a romantic relationship and wish to disclose certain aspects about yourself. You possess genuine concern for this individual's well-being and aspire to maintain their companionship, yet you harbor a fear that by revealing your vulnerable side, they may distance themselves. However, an individual of importance should inherently possess the desire to understand your thoughts and perspectives.

You wish to inquire with your supervisor at the workplace regarding a salary increase. You have concerns regarding the lack of serious consideration, potential termination, or disruption of established procedures. However, the most unfavorable response from your manager would be a straightforward denial. It can be challenging to expose oneself, but refraining from doing so only leads to self-inflicted harm.

The apprehension preceding an event is consistently more intense than the actual object of one's fear. It is readily comprehensible the potential outcomes, whether they materialize or not. However frequently have your most dreaded nightmares materialized?

Utilizing emotional intelligence in the resolution of conflicts

By possessing the ability to discern and comprehend both your own emotional state and the emotions of others, you will find it more convenient to effectively address and resolve interpersonal conflicts that may arise. Applying emotional intelligence within the context of conflict resolution entails following these outlined procedures:

Determine the nature of your emotional state.

It is crucial to garner an understanding of one's emotions during conflicts, as this comprehension facilitates the identification of appropriate solutions for addressing workplace or other life-related issues. Suppose you found yourself in a professional scenario wherein you encountered difficulty in resolving a disagreement pertaining to the completion of a daily task schedule. One may experience feelings characterized not by anger, but rather by concern, as a result of being unsure about how to fulfill all the designated tasks and lacking comprehension of how to address specific challenges as they arise.

You must adequately assess and manage your emotions, refraining from fixating on any potential feelings of anger. By comprehending your genuine concerns, you will prevent the involvement of any complexities in the conflict resolution process.

Organize your thoughts in accordance with your emotions.

It is imperative that you consider your approach to verbal expression in accordance with your thought process. It is imperative that you refrain from utilizing any expressions or cues indicative of anger. In lieu of that, you must categorize your emotions according to the level of distress or apprehension you experience regarding your potential inability to accomplish specific tasks within a designated timeframe.

Express your emotions to the individual.

It is necessary for you to confront your emotions by engaging in dialogue with someone regarding the current circumstances. Regarding the schedule, you may engage in a discussion expressing your apprehension regarding your ability to accomplish a particular task within the allocated timeframe. It is imperative to engage in discussions pertaining to concerns regarding one's ability to execute a task with optimal quality. You may choose to articulate your concerns to someone, thereby facilitating the development of a resolution that will guarantee your successful completion of tasks within a designated timeframe.

Volume III: The Art of Effective Writing

1. Keep it simple

Keep your writing simple. The objective of your written communication is to effectively communicate the accurate message. The objective is not to showcase your lexicon to others. Alternatively, one may choose to compose a work of prose or poetry that is discerned and admired by only a select few. The objective is to accomplish the task.

I previously presented a report to my superior. My superior contacted me to express that it was indistinct. Subsequently, he became preoccupied with other tasks. I was left uncertain - I lacked clarity on whether I had received acknowledgement or criticism. Alternatively, what course of action was expected of me? I grabbed a dictionary.

Nebulous means confusing. Consequently, I dedicated my efforts to enhancing the clarity of the report, all while pondering the reason behind my superior's omission of acknowledging its perplexing nature.

In general, the utilization of elementary vocabulary is capable of effectively communicating the intended message. Why burden yourself and others by employing complex vocabulary? Keep it simple.

Use simple words. You are not engaged in a vocabulary challenge or a crossword championship.

Avoid being verbose. Omit unnecessary words. The statement 'She is very beautiful' is synonymous with 'She possesses great beauty'. The utilization of the word 'very' is not contributing significantly to the content. Drop it.

Please refrain from composing lengthy paragraphs when a succinct sentence would be sufficient. Recall the longstanding proverb that affirms the incapacity of a sword to fulfill the role of a needle. Use what is required.

Please avoid excessive expansion of the background story. The reader is an individual with a hectic schedule. Life is short. Promptly address the central objective.

Do refrain from employing colloquial language or acronyms, particularly if your intended readership lacks a substantive knowledge in the field.

Use small sentences. Please refrain from composing lengthy paragraphs that merge multiple sentences using conjunctions such as 'and,' 'or,' and ','. The conveyed message shall become obscured.

2. Use bullets

In particular, when it comes to communicating within an office setting, employing bullet points and numbered lists is recommended. They make a difference. Observe the two sentences presented below.

The 7 fundamental principles adhered to by exceptionally proficient writers are as follows: strive for simplicity, master the art of storytelling, harness the potency of summaries, ponder over your intentions and motivations, engage in meticulous editing, and diligently practice reading aloud prior to submitting your work.

Listed below are the seven principles that distinguish exceptionally productive writers:

Keep it simple

Art of storytelling

Power of summaries

What are your desires and the underlying reasons behind them?

Edit...edit...edit

Read aloud before submission

Look at the difference. The utilization of bullets and numbering lends an air of organization and clarity to your work, effectively conveying the intended message.

Spiritual Health

As previously observed, the World Health Organization (WHO) acknowledges the inclusion of spiritual health as a constituent that significantly contributes to an individual's overall well-being. This subject receives limited discussion due to its inherent religious associations. Nevertheless, should the attainment of elevated levels of overall well-being prove unattainable in the absence of a harmonious interplay between all dimensions, namely the mind, body, and spirit, it is imperative that spirit is duly incorporated. This discourse does not stem from a singular religious point of view or esoteric inclination. Instead, it endeavors to comprehend, through a humanistic lens, the essence of spiritual well-being and its interconnectedness with other facets of health. In terms of a philosophical framework, spiritual well-being takes precedence over empirical evidence and instead draws upon a collection of anecdotal occurrences that are consistently recounted, gradually gaining credibility.

It is alleged that spiritual well-being bestows upon individuals a raison d'être and significance to their existence, by ensuring a sense of completeness through the adherence to a steadfast set of principles, ethics, and values. These convictions are presumed to serve as the foundation for the appreciation of aesthetics and a sense of interconnectedness with fellow beings, granting feelings of affection, bliss, optimism, and contentment.

It is widely recognized that individuals who possess spiritual well-being exhibit a harmonious framework of beliefs that effectively elucidate their perception of reality. These convictions need not be of a religious nature; nonetheless, they address inquiries such as: "What is the purpose of my existence?"; "What brings significance and contentment to my life?"; "How can I attain happiness and fulfillment?" While responding to these queries, every individual attains a heightened sense of objective and significance in their being, as well as a direction towards personal contentment. This spiritual health viewpoint offers individuals a coherent framework of ethical principles, convictions, and behavioral guidance, fostering a positive sense of self. Conversations centeredaround spirituality commonly encompass notions such as benevolence, altruism, veracity, rectitude, and social interconnectedness. Numerous studies have confirmed the crucial role these principles play in promoting psychological and physiological well-being. Take a moment to ponder the detrimental alternatives. As an illustration, an antonym for selflessness could be synonymous with self-indulgence. Individuals who possess a predisposition to engage in hedonistic activities are more susceptible to developing addictive tendencies, as well as experiencing an increased sense of vacuity.

Interpersonal communication serves as a visible expression of one's spiritual well-being. In a state of optimal well-being, individuals engage in interpersonal communication marked by uprightness, moral rectitude, reliance, benevolence, and an authentic regard for others. There is a clear and undeniable correlation between the desire for love and acceptance and one's spiritual well-being. Similar to physical and mental well-being, this facet of health is cultivated during early stages of life, specifically infancy and childhood, within the framework of a compassionate family. An awareness of affection and acknowledgement is fundamental to cultivating a positive sense of self. This self-confidence is inherent to the perspectives on reality, principles, and moral codes that are imparted to us during the early stages of our development. Individuals possessing a well-nourished psyche perceive the splendor and interrelatedness present within existence. They harbinger a disposition characterized by inclusiveness and open-mindedness towards others, alongside an enhanced level of self-compassion and acceptance.

The concept of spiritual well-being can be intricately interconnected with one's mental and physical well-being. Bestowing upon an individual a sense of life purpose and a profound, overarching significance to their existence, this can serve as the foundation for guiding principles, deeply-held values, and ethical convictions, while also evoking sentiments of affection, tranquility, optimism, and contentment. A robust state of mental well-being can therefore be discerned through sound and wholesome interpersonal interactions.

Social Factors

Societal transformations are occurring at a swift pace, and their manifestations are readily discernible. Any alteration inevitably entails a multitude of accompanying factors. The present societal landscape is characterized by a vigorous pursuit of self-interest and a consequential prevalence of intense competition, alongside underlying feelings of uncertainty and insecurity. It has significantly contributed to the isolation of children in one area. The period of isolation is not a punitive measure, but rather a necessary course of action at present. The prevalence of cable television, internet, and social media platforms is substantial in this regard.

The proliferation of social media platforms dates back slightly more than two decades. The true surge in popularity occurred subsequent to the inception of the Facebook era, and presently there exist an abundant array of websites of similar nature that aim to captivate youngsters.

In the current era, it would prove challenging to motivate a child to engage in outdoor activities, as children are increasingly allocating greater amounts of time towards socializing on the internet. Their primary emphasis lies in engaging with social networks in the virtual realm, as opposed to direct, tangible interactions, due to their ability to disconnect from the virtual world at any given moment.

This news is considerably more concerning than it initially appears, as children who boast a large online social circle might not even have a handful of reliable acquaintances. Consequently, this fosters an illusory sense of self-assurance that can prove perilous when they transition to real-life professional environments.

Although social media platforms provide an interactive experience, they are demanding an excessive amount of time from young individuals, thereby imparting a potentially illusory sense of security.

Acquiring social skills can prove challenging, even for children of this nature as they mature. The complexities of the world extend beyond the simple act of unfriending or blocking a person with merely a click.

Mental Health Issues

Various mental health conditions, such as depression and social anxiety disorders, can contribute to individuals leading a solitary existence. Individuals of this nature are experiencing significant internal turmoil, which can result in challenges when attempting to navigate and adapt to the external realm.

Without receiving adequate exposure and support, individuals may encounter significant challenges in honing their social skills.

Shoulders specifically

The configuration of our shoulders influences the perceptions that others hold of us, as it signals our well-being and emotional state, while also serving as a crucial instrument in our communication endeavors.

In a comparable manner to the chest, the positioning of the shoulders is an overt indicator of body language that can be readily discerned. When the shoulders are aligned in a posterior position with the chest protruding forward, it typically signifies a state of confidence. If the shoulders are observed to be anteriorly positioned with the body exhibiting a hunched posture, it can be indicative of diminished levels of confidence or self-esteem. Additionally, it may serve as evidence of a prevailing sense of dejection or melancholy. Typically, individuals exhibit a lower placement of their shoulders when they experience a sense of relaxation, whereas a raised position of the shoulders is observed when they feel tense or anxious.

A gesture characterized by a lifting and lowering of the shoulders, commonly denotes a lack of knowledge or inability to provide assistance in a certain manner. Partially owing to their conspicuous placement on the physique, robust and pliable shoulders can effectively convey an impression of liveliness and innate harmony. In contrast, should the shoulders exhibit weakness and restricted movement, potentially attributable to the frequent assumption of a hunched position, it may give off the perception of the individual experiencing depression.

Gestures

Gestures encompass actions involving the hands, arms, fingers, head, and legs. These actions can be either voluntary or inadvertent. There exist a multitude of diverse interpretations when considering the various gestures made with one's arms. Engaging in a conversation while crossing one's arms, whether in a standing, sitting, or even walking position, is generally perceived as an unfriendly gesture. This could indicate that they possess a narrow mindset and are unlikely to be receptive towards the perspective put forth by the speaker. An alternative arm movement that signifies apprehension and a dearth of assurance is the act of crossing one arm over the other.

According to the authors Barbara Pease and Allan Pease, as stated in their publication The Definitive Book of Body Language, the action of shrugging the shoulders is observed universally. A frequently employed gesture to communicate one's lack of comprehension is the act of shrugging. Further explanation reveals that the gesture encompasses three fundamental elements. The individual showcased open palms as a means to convey a lack of concealed objects or intentions within the hands, employed a posture with slightly hunched shoulders to provide protection to the vulnerable throat area, and exemplified a lifted brow, a universally recognized symbol of receptive greeting.

Gestures often serve as indications of the creator's emotional state. Tightly gripped hands can be perceived as a manifestation of stress or anger, whereas hands at ease indicate a sense of confidence and self-assuredness. The act of wringing one's hands connotes a state of unease and restlessness in an individual.

Moreover, hand gestures are commonly utilized to exemplify words and convey the state of one's mental and physical health. In certain cultural contexts, gesturing with the index finger is regarded as socially acceptable. Nevertheless, gesturing towards an individual could be interpreted as aggressive in certain cultural contexts. An illustrative example would be that Hindus perceive the act of pointing fingers as a display of disrespect. Alternatively, they elevate their palms while extending their fingers to indicate the direction. Similarly, in countries such as the United States, South Africa, France, Lebanon, and Germany, the thumbs-up gesture is commonly employed to signify approval or affirmation. Nevertheless, this very gesture is deemed disrespectful in other countries including Iran, Bangladesh, and Thailand, where it carries the same offensive connotation as the internationally recognized middle finger gesture.

It is not feasible to promptly rectify an individual's initial impression once it has been formed. Nevertheless, with the passage of time, it is possible to gradually acquaint others with one's true nature. One of the most effective strategies to address misunderstandings, particularly when they arise early in a conversation, is to present a substantial body of evidence demonstrating the inaccuracies in the individual's perspective. Indeed, it is important to acquaint them with every occurrence that contradicts their perception of the truth regarding your character.

This could potentially require a significant amount of time, as individuals have a tendency to perceive attempts to influence their perception of oneself. Nevertheless, if one consistently presents compelling evidence to the contrary, it is possible for an individual's cognitive framework to undergo rewiring, subsequently leading to a shift in their perspective. By offering a substantial accumulation of evidence that exceeds one's initial perception of you, you will generate ample contradictory information. The individual will gradually experience an enhanced sense of reassurance from the new information, consequently prompting a contemplation of their initial evaluation towards you.

6. Please expedite the process of reaching a clear and concise conclusion.

Please prioritize accuracy: You are not Beyoncé, therefore refrain from engaging in excessive movement or digressions while addressing a particular point or matter. Engaging in lengthy digressions, excessive pauses, stuttering, adopting verbosity, and other such tendencies can cause frustration to the interlocutor and heighten the likelihood of miscommunication. For effective communication, it is advisable to express your thoughts concisely rather than indulging in meandering discourse. In the event that articulating your thoughts becomes challenging, it would be advisable to refrain and instead seek a more opportune moment to engage in communication when you feel more equipped to convey your message effectively.

Avoid using unnecessary embellishments when conveying your thoughts; instead, opt for brevity, precision, and efficacy. Indulging in circumlocution will detract from the efficacy of your intended message. It is advisable to refrain from leaving others in a state of uncertainty when discussing matters of significance. Politely inquire whether they have comprehended the intended message without conveying any sense of condescension or patronization. Do you comprehend the information that has been presented? Are you comprehending the message I am attempting to articulate? Here are a few inquiries you may pose to assess the other individual's comprehension. Exhibit patience and await a response from them. Please endeavor to navigate the issue.

I have encountered several individuals who frequently display a tendency to engage in excessive and uncontrolled verbal expression. They make various statements insincerely. This is setting the stage for a multitude of emotional distress. By uttering words devoid of sincerity, one lays the foundation for confusion and skepticism to infiltrate every aspect of communication. Exemplify integrity and uphold your commitments. Misinterpretation is significantly influenced by the surrounding circumstances. It is impacted by various factors, such as the identity of the individual involved, the dynamic of your relationship with them, and the emotional context established between both parties. Nonetheless, it is imperative to always communicate with sincerity and refrain from expressing thoughts or intentions that deviate from the truth.

Example Conversation

Take this illustrative dialogue between a marital pair discussing the prospect of relocation. This exemplary dialogue exemplifies the adept utilization of the four fundamental facets of efficacious communication.

Husband: I would appreciate the opportunity to converse with you about a matter that my supervisor brought up earlier today. Please observe the use of the term "discuss." This phrasing is preferable to "talk" as it conveys the notion of an open dialogue rather than a mere dissemination of information.

Spouse: My employer is currently contemplating offering me a promotion. However, it would necessitate relocation to a different locality. If I were to accept it, the event would occur within the following two months.

Spouse: I am opposed to the idea of relocating our children during the ongoing academic term. Could it wait?

Husband: I comprehend your reluctance to relocate the children presently, however, I am uncertain if they will exhibit patience. Please observe the implementation of active listening.

Husband: Apart from that, do you have any qualms? What are your thoughts? He assumes a stance wherein his arms are gently extended and his hands are positioned a moderate distance apart. The individual's nonverbal cues are encouraging the expression of her viewpoints." "The individual's physical gestures are fostering an environment that welcomes her insights." "Her opinions are being actively solicited through the use of nonverbal communication.

Wife: It would be greatly advantageous for you to progress in your professional endeavors and attain enhanced financial security. Perhaps we could collaborate to find a resolution regarding the educational aspect.

During the course of this exchange, the husband should maintain a tone of voice that is open and inviting. This is not an autocracy, but rather a transparent deliberation regarding the potential relocation. It is crucial to effectively communicate this message through the appropriate use of tone and body language in order to mitigate potential conflicts.

All the valuable recommendations pertain to the utilization of one's cognitive faculties during the act of attentive listening. That, undoubtedly, is the fundamental issue at hand. Nonetheless, it is insufficient to simply assert that one's cognitive faculties must be fully engrossed in auditory reception, that one's perceptions should not be influenced by irrelevant emotions, and that the level of mental exertion must align with the degree of difficulty or intricacy presented by the speaker's discourse. Hence, simply asserting that the listener should possess the intellectual courtesy to assume that the information being conveyed is sufficiently captivating and pertinent to deserve attention falls short. While the speaker's ability to validate that assumption may be uncertain, it is advisable to approach their perspective with an initial stance of open-mindedness and attentiveness. What additional information should be provided in order to establish affirmative principles that can be adopted and practiced to cultivate the habit of active listening?

I would like to express that the guidelines for successful reading are essentially identical to those of my response. That outcome is to be expected. The two processes exhibit similarities with respect to the cognitive demands imposed on the mind.

Regardless of the circumstance, the recipient's cognition, whether it be the reader or listener, must ascertain the underlying concept that is being conveyed beyond the literal expression of words. It is imperative to tackle the obstacles hindering understanding caused by language. The lexicon employed by the speaker or writer rarely, if ever, aligns with the lexicon used by the listener or reader. The second option must consistently endeavor to attain a significance that can be expressed through various arrangements of words. The acceptance of the speaker by the audience is equally important as the acceptance of the writer by the reader. This necessitates identifying the essence of the idea irrespective of its expression in verbal communication.

When engaging in the act of listening or reading, it is crucial to pay heed to the assertions that convey the fundamental concepts that the speaker or writer is endeavoring to convey. Not all spoken or written content carries equal significance. There is a dearth of truly substantial statements presented in the majority of discussions, regardless of whether they are verbal or written. The recipient, similar to the reader, must identify and emphasize these elements mentally, differentiating them from other intervening, transitional, or simply explanatory and illustrative contextual statements.

The speech that is being heard, analogous to any written composition, is a cohesive entity comprising various components. If a speech or presentation has value, its arrangement (the organization of its components to achieve a unified whole) and progression (the logical flow from one element to another) will be evident and coherent. Consequently, the receiver, similar to the recipient, is required to make a conscious effort in order to discern the connections and order of the individual components that make up the entirety.

The orator, akin to the author, commences with a comprehensive and controlling intent or purpose that dictates the substance and manner of the discourse or presentation. It is imperative for both the reader and listener to promptly recognize the primary objective or purpose of this overarching aim. This will enable them to effectively differentiate between elements of substantial importance and those of marginal significance within the discourse they are attempting to comprehend.

Comprehending the intended message of the speaker, perceiving their mode of expression, and evaluating the rationale and supporting arguments put forth to garner acceptance for the speaker's intended conclusions are indispensable for adept listening, just as they are for proficient reading. However, they are invariably inadequate. It is of utmost importance to form one's own personal perspective, either in agreement or disagreement, with regards to any information acquired through reading or listening.

One might find themselves unable to do so due to a lack of sufficient comprehension of what has been spoken, making it difficult to form a justified position of agreement or disagreement. One additional factor that could warrant postponing the expression of agreement or disagreement is the absence of sufficient clarifications or supporting arguments. Regardless of the circumstances, the discerning listener, much like the discerning reader, ought to postpone forming a judgment and revisit the subject at a later point.

In my publication titled How to Read a Book, I present a comprehensive set of instructions pertaining to the process of reading a book which, based on its substance and composition, justifies a meticulous approach. Initially, there existed a set of criteria for evaluating the book's comprehensive framework and the systematic organization of its components. It is imperative for an individual to possess the ability to articulate the overarching theme and the contribution of each individual component in order to elucidate the overall significance of the book.

Tell Me In Mimes How I Am Feeling

Essential supplies required for this activity include paper, markers, and a blackboard.

The minimum required number of individuals is 20 and 25 individuals, respectively.

Duration: Approximately 30 to 45 minutes

Children and adolescents diagnosed with Asperger's syndrome exhibit substantial challenges in perceiving and comprehending the emotions of others. Oftentimes, their apparent lack of concern is not indicative of their indifference, but rather stems from their limited capacity to discern and appropriately respond to these emotions.

For this rationale, it is imperative to concentrate efforts on developing this acknowledgement in order to enhance interpersonal dynamics within the given setting.

The objective of the activity is to arrange all participants of the group in circular formations, with the purpose of portraying distinct emotional states through the utilization of modeling techniques.

The child or adolescent diagnosed with Asperger's syndrome is a designated participant. The leader of the group selects an emotion to portray via the art of mime, and subsequently elucidates the situation to the group by means of an illustration. The individual selected as the ASchild shall endeavor to make a conjecture.

He/she may seek insights from his/her colleagues and, amidst varying perspectives, attempt to discern the depicted emotions.

After successfully discerning the emotion, he/she will be prompted to endeavor in creating a representation for the remaining participants to conjecture.

Lastly, a brief contemplation is presented regarding the significance of having awareness and empathy towards the emotions of others, in order to foster meaningful interpersonal connections that benefit all individuals involved.

8

We perused a narrative.

The required items for this particular setup include a narrative, along with visual aids in the form of illustrative posters.

Minimum number of individuals required: 20 and 25 individuals.

Duration: Approximately 30 to 45 minutes

To address this aspect, a reading comprehension exercise will be created with the aim of enabling the child or adolescent with Autism Spectrum to perceptively connect their emotions with the content they engage in.

Attendees are requested to form a circular arrangement, seated in close proximity. The reading is initiated by the leader, with utmost attention demanded from all participants. Notably, the narrative intricately revolves around the emotional state of every character.

The objective is for the child or adolescent with Asperger's syndrome to comprehend that individuals who are not on the spectrum also have the ability to perceive and express emotions.

After the completion of the reading, a sequence of inquiries will be presented to the participants, pertaining directly to the emotions conveyed by the characters.

When it is the child's turn, he or she will be required to empathize with each character individually in order to discern their respective emotions.

Subsequently, a signal system comprising a variety of hues and signage featuring emotional correlations to the respective traffic light colors will be furnished. Attendees will be required to individually choose each item and appropriately position it within the traffic light according to its respective color.

Ultimately, there will be an assurance that all individuals within the group have successfully comprehended and recognized the range of emotions experienced by humans, and will be guided towards effectively managing them.

To address the challenge of establishing social connections, group dynamics are employed.

The matter of cultivating social relationships appears to hold negligible significance among children and adolescents diagnosed with Asperger's Syndrome.

However, the fact of the matter is that they are individuals who lack the necessary resources to engage in social interaction, let alone create an environment of mutual confidence that would foster deeper personal connections and cultivate friendships.

This can lead to a state of frustration, thereby provoking both aggression and anxiety. Proper guidance should be provided to navigate this internal conflict and facilitate the enhancement of relationships.

As per the Diagnostic and Statistical Manual of Mental Disorders (DSM-5), a notable trait observed in individuals with Asperger syndrome is the lack of inherent inclination to spontaneously engage in the sharing of enjoyment, interests, and goals with others.

Executing a meticulously structured task can have a profound impact in establishing environments wherein individuals discern a sense of value and perceive that their personal priorities hold significance for all parties involved.

Presentations

30. Be yourself. The objective of your presentation is not to achieve flawless perfection, but rather to establish genuine connections and effectively convey your message.

31. It is advisable to condense your presentation to three key points." "It would be most beneficial to limit your presentation to three primary points." "For optimal results, it is recommended to focus your presentation on three major points. The majority of individuals have the capacity to recall solely three key points. This is not an incontrovertible fact, however ... By devoting your energy and time to the achievement of your three primary

objectives, it is more likely that you will successfully conclude your presentation with all intended goals accomplished.

32. Make a concerted effort to commit the opening of your presentation to memory. The peak of anxiety is experienced during the initial phase of a presentation. Exert utmost control over your introduction to effectively engage your audience and ensure a composed and confident delivery that leaves no room for nervousness.

33. One effective method to hold the attention of your audience is by actively engaging them. On average, adults possess an attention span ranging from five to seven minutes... or less!

34. Silence is powerful. Pause periodically. This exhibits a sense of tranquility and self-assurance.

Feedback

35. Please ensure that all individuals under your supervision possess a comprehensive comprehension of the

performance expectations set for them. Effective feedback results from individuals having a clear understanding of the criteria by which their performance is being evaluated.

36. Cultivate the practice of providing regular feedback to each member of your team on a weekly basis. If you have a tendency to forget, make it a point to establish a reminder on your calendar.

37. Request input regarding your assessment. Seek evaluations from others regarding your nonverbal cues (appearance, actions, etc.) in addition to obtaining verbal input.

38. Seek and implement input from others. Do not postpone the gathering of performance feedback until your performance appraisal.

39. Enlist individuals within your circle of influence to collaborate as allies in your pursuit of ongoing enhancement. Consistently seek input on the perception of your image and reputation.

40. Be concise and specific. Exercise caution when employing words and phrases that possess multiple interpretations, thereby leading to potential divergences among individuals (e.g., typically, intermittently, significantly, infrequently, etc.).

41. Tailor the acknowledgment you offer. Inquire from each individual within your team regarding the most effective manner in which you can manifest your gratitude towards them. Subsequently, offer a range of options that cater to varying preferences and individuals' unique needs.

42. One should never make the assumption that others comprehend what is being expressed verbally or in writing; it is essential to verify. Kindly request them to articulate their comprehension of your message. This will afford you the opportunity to elucidate and rectify any misapprehensions.

43. Implement a policy of transparent communication with yourself and others, whereby unexpected information or developments are minimized. Transform the act of concealing adverse information into the gravest transgression.

44. Please refrain from engaging in the practice of accumulating and retaining information for personal gain, exhibiting behaviors typically associated with a powerful and influential individual. Solicit input from every individual within your team, encouraging them to determine the specific type and quantity of information that would significantly contribute to their effectiveness, and ensure that their requirements are fulfilled.

Chapter 6 Summary

The cultivation of self-assurance is a crucial aspect to be developed in order to enhance one's conversational skills.

● The key lies in the power of mental resilience, and the ability to transform one's mindset solely rests in your control. An illustration of how this can be achieved lies in the utilization of either constructive self-affirmations or the practice of meditation. However, it is essential to identify a method that resonates most effectively with your individuality to harness optimal outcomes.

● Give yourself congratulations for a job well done. ● Extend commendations to yourself for achieving success. ● Offer yourself a well-deserved pat on the back after accomplishing something commendable. ● Acknowledge and celebrate your own achievements. It is not obligatory for the accomplishments to be of substantial importance. The small accomplishments you have attained throughout the day that elicit a sense of "I did it!" are commendable. Recognizing one's achievements in a proficient manner can contribute to the gradual development of self-assurance.

● Recognize the specific areas that require enhancement and compile a list of recommendations to effectively address those areas. It is not imperative for the goals to be of substantial magnitude. Commence with attainable objectives that you are capable of accomplishing, in order to evade feelings of discouragement.

● Compile an inventory of your aptitudes that serve as substantiation of the valuable attributes you possess for potential utilization. These elements might have eluded your attention or contemplation in the past, yet leveraging their potential can aid in the restoration and cultivation of confidence.

● Allocate adequate time to practicing personal hygiene and tending to your attire. It is essential to cultivate a sense of self-assurance by taking the time to ensure personal well-being prior to departing from your residence.

The LEEP framework for Managing Anger from External Sources

There are four factors that frequently give rise to a breakdown in our ability to assert ourselves. The four aforementioned aspects are acknowledged within the framework of the LEEP model. Conceived by Dr.Klenke, this conceptual framework incorporates Logos, which represents our intellect, Eros, which encompasses our feelings, Ethos, which governs our ethical principles, and Pathos, which encompasses the various elements that contribute to this state of dysfunction. Allow us to delve into the intricate details of each of these contributing factors in order to enhance our ability to effectively cope with anger from others.

LOGOS: This constituent regards each person as a cognitive being. This implies that our cognitive faculties can be employed to tackle diverse circumstances in life. We possess the capacity to furnish sound justifications for all our endeavors and demonstrate the ability to adapt in accordance with diverse circumstances. The Logos component pertains to the art of persuasion through the utilization of compelling empirical evidence.

ETHOS: Each individual harbors a collection of moral obligations that dictate every facet of their existence. This ethical component enables us to make choices that are uplifting and imbued with meaning. Each one of us adheres to specific principles that shape our responses in various circumstances. By maintaining these values in our approach towards anger, it is highly probable that we will establish appropriate and accountable reparations.

The Eros element represents the convergence of emotion and intellect. This element facilitates our ability to approach challenging circumstances with enthusiasm and optimism, despite their potentially discomforting nature. Eros pertains to the intrinsic sentiment commonly known as our intuitive perception, enabling us to navigate through various circumstances. These emotions, namely love, compassion, resilience, and empathy, are given due consideration within this particular component. Taking into consideration the EROS component, it is probable that we will cultivate heightened receptivity and tolerance when addressing anger.

PATHOS: Pathos pertains to the missteps that result in unfavorable circumstances. It is only through our acceptance of this situation that we can facilitate alterations in our behavior. Occasionally, the compulsion for flawlessness and correctness can propel us to become overly zealous and confront situations in an unyielding manner.

Implementing Assertiveness In Your Circumstances

Being assertive means the same thing in any situation. But, different circumstances also require you to be assertive in different ways. Every situation may not require you to say a distinct no. Every situation may not require you to repeat your stand, etc. So, be aware of what sort of assertiveness needs to be applied. Given here are a few instances that will take you through how you can be assertive in different situations.

At work

Assertiveness at work is a very important thing. It makes you a more efficient, honest and a reliable resource for the company and a great colleague to have. Your assertiveness will ultimately benefit the company.

Responding to Compliments

When you are complimented for your efforts or for the way you look, if you tend to feel inadequate, then, you are not assertive. Assertiveness requires you to be graceful about the compliments of your skills and not be guilty of being complacent. Responding to compliments is a little unnatural for a lot of people. So, whenever you receive a compliment try to take it in positively by enquiring about it. When you are told that something about you is nice, respond with a smile and a simply 'thank you'. Further, you can always ask them what exactly about you did they like. Also, make sure you find at least one thing from their compliments to agree with.

Being an Assertive Boss

While most bosses from around the planet are guilty of being either aggressive or passive, very few of them know how to be an assertive boss. Being a boss is not a license for you to ill-treat your subordinates. Assertive bosses make sure that they value their staff as key to the company's success. Assertive bosses are aware that while their position gives them the authority, they have to earn their respect.

Being an Assertive Employee

It is very important for you to be aware of your personal rights. Each time a colleague takes a leave of absence or piles up his work load, it is not your duty to clean the mess. You are responsible for your position in the firm. And, your behavior is detrimental to your success and growth in the company.

- Say, "NO" when you are unable to do a job.

- Refuse to a request if you do not to want to shoulder extra responsibility.

- Be responsible for everything that you are assigned.

- Your growth in a company is your responsibility.

- Your failures are also your responsibility. Do not blame anybody else.

- Use fogging and breaking record techniques to be assertive.

- Contribute ideas, voice your opinions and share your feelings whenever you feel like.

- Ask for help when you need it. It does not make you incompetent.

At Home

Being assertive at home is a whole different thing. At home refusing a request maybe the hardest task. But, it is important to remember that saying, "Yes" to everything does not make you the best parent or son or daughter or wife or husband. You do not have to suppress your feeling or resort to aggression when met with a situation. You must express your feeling, opinion, and view as much as the next member of the family. You do not step down for others to be accommodated. Being assertive at home will also influence your mind to behave similarly in the outside world.

Being an Assertive Parent

Being an assertive parent is the best gift you can give your child. It is an excellent way of imparting discipline in your child without yelling at him. When you are assertive, you do not have to ignore his mistakes either. And, this makes you feel stronger and more in control of your life an parent. You will see that being assertive is making you a better parent.

- State very clearly what is expected of your child.
- Do not harass him with unwanted details. Be precise.
- If you say No, be firm.
- Do not insult your child. Convey what you want to in a polite way.
- Do not indulge in physical expression of anger. Instead state very clearly opinion and feelings.
- Do not be afraid to correct him.

Being an Assertive Wife/Husband

Being a good life partner does not require you to say yes to everything. And, being a good partner does not allow you to be aggressive. But, for the sake of keeping harmony one should not be taken for a ride in the relationship while other person gains complete control. Both are equal partners in the relationship and for its healthy functioning.

- Refuse clearly and firmly. State the background for your decision.

- Be open and honest with your opinions, feelings and views. It need not always sit well with the other person.

- Be open to the possibility of being subjected to a similar openness in their communication.

- Aggression of any form does not mean that you are in control.

- Mind your words while expressing yourself.

- Do not apologize for refusing a request.

Visualize Your Ideal Future

What better way to find your passion than visualizing your ideal life. The secret is to keep things as realistic as possible. We tend to overestimate what we're capable of doing in a year, yet we underestimate what we can achieve in 10 years (Hreha, n.d).

Humans, for the most part, are very impatient and we want to see impressive results instantly. That is why our visualizations are usually limited to the first year and often contains success that isn't achievable. Unfortunately, when the year comes to an end and we didn't get the results we envisioned, we feel discouraged and lose confidence. This demotivation often leads to us giving up on our dreams.

I learned an important trick to avoid "over-selling" my abilities in short-term visualizations—I don't do short-term visualizations! I only envision myself three to five years ahead. I also try my best to be true to my abilities and what I can achieve in this timeframe.

It's not always easy to envision what my dream life looks like. When this happens, I pick up a pen and paper and write down what comes to mind. As long as you're thinking about your future, it doesn't matter if you play it out in your head like a movie or write it down in bullet form. What matters is that you're taking the time to discover what you want.

Here are step-by-step instructions for visualizing what you want in life:

Find a quiet place to sit where there are no distractions.

Imagine yourself in three years time. Where are you? What are you doing?

Close your eyes and visualize if you'd like.

Now, imagine what you consider a perfect life for you.

Think of the life you want as if there are no limits.

Don't rush the process. Envision all aspects of the future you, your financial success, relationships, career, health, spirituality, etc.

Do this at least once a week to keep those goals at the forefront of your mind when making choices. If those goals change as time goes by, that is completely okay too!

Go on a Journey of Self-Discovery

You're an expert when it comes to your life. So, why not ask yourself some important questions to help you discover what you want to do with your life? The mind is a wonderful thing, and when you ask questions, it will look for the answers.

Some self-discovery questions I recommend you ask include:

- Who do I want to be?
- Who do I have a high regard for?
- Am I happy with the job I have right now?

- If I had all the money I needed, what would I spend my time on?
- What are my strong points?
- What does an ideal day in a perfect life look like?
- What makes me happy?

Write down your answers and keep them with you. I still keep a copy of my answers. On days when I feel low and find myself questioning my decisions, I read through them again to make myself feel better. It works because it reminds me how far I've come and where I'm heading.

Just one more thing; don't overthink it. Limit the time you have to answer the questions. That way, you don't have time to argue away your original response and change it into a more 'acceptable' one.

Trust Your Intuition

It's frightening how other's opinions can mute our inner voices. Sadly, we end up dancing to their drums and don't live authentically. One way to safeguard against this is to pay close attention to your instinct. In other words, follow your heart.

Regrettably, many of us have lost the ability to tap into our intuition. You will need to re-learn how to identify your inner voice. Here are some tips on how to do just that:

Search Out Tranquility

It's challenging to listen to what your heart has to say when you're distracted by things in your environment. I recommend you go for a walk; find a place where there is little noise and other distractions. If that's not an option, switch off your phone and lock yourself in a room with a tranquil atmosphere. Maybe try out meditation, even if it's something you've never done before.

When you're alone with your thoughts and in a peaceful state, your intuition is stronger than usual and you may experience a 'eureka' moment.

Question Everything

Society and your culture impose so many rules on you. Often, if you want to live your life, you'll have to be a rule breaker. So, question everything. Do you have to get married? Do you have to have kids? Why should you not attempt to become the Chief Operating Officer of a Fortune 500 company? Why can't you take a leave from your job, rent out your residence and spend a few months traveling the world?

You see, it is your life. You only get one and you should do what you can to live it in such a way so you're happy; not based on what your parents, family, partner, or anyone else says. Society has 'trained' us to believe there are limited options. To follow your heart, you have to listen to your intuition and question everything.

Don't Ignore Your Body

Our bodies have the ability to tell us several things. When you're tired, you'll yawn, your eyes will get heavy, and you may find it difficult to focus. That's your body signaling that it is time to get some rest. Similarly, your body will let you know when you need to connect with your inner self.

When I am overly anxious and feel out of sorts, I know it is my body's way of telling me I need to take a moment to look inward. You get some insightful answers to questions you don't know you even had when you listen to your inner self.

Practice saying no

Despite the fact it made me unhappy, I kept saying yes to what made me feel uncomfortable and simply wasted my time. Initially, I forced myself to say no and learned this phrase: "No, sorry, I cannot do it". I told myself: "Tiana, every time someone asks you to do something you don't want to do, don't think, just say this". The idea behind is somewhat similar to a phrase: "Fake it till you make it". So I was faking it with "No, sorry, I cannot do it" till I was confident enough to provide some more explanation as to why I cannot. So, if they asked: "Why?" I'd answer: "I don't feel like doing it", "I've already got other plans", "I've got to do something else". If it's work, then of course you need to provide a legit reason.

Don't hesitate — be direct. If an explanation is appropriate, keep it brief.

Rehearse what you would say before the situation arises

The scripting assertive technique can help here. It allows you to prepare what you want to say in advance using a four-pronged approach that helps you build the conversation:

- **The event**

Tell the other person exactly how you see the situation or problem. "Peter, the production costs this month are 23 percent higher than average".

- **Your feelings**

Describe how you feel about the situation and express your emotions clearly. "This frustrates me and makes me feel like you don't understand or appreciate how important financial controls are in the company".

- **Your needs**

Tell the other person exactly what you need from her so that she doesn't have to guess. "I need you to be honest with me and let me know when we start going significantly over budget on anything".

- **The consequences**

Describe the positive impact that your request will have for the other person or the company if your needs are met successfully. "If you do this, we will be in a good position to hit our targets and may get a better end-of-year bonus".

If it's challenging to say what you want or think, practice typical scenarios you encounter and know what to say when the situation arises again. If you're now thinking that it's silly to replay situations in your head, it's something that I have done because it does help to be prepared and not get stuck in a moment without knowing what to say or acting the way you typically do. Say what you want to say out loud and be convinced. Try not to stammer. It may help to write it out first, too, so you can practice from a script.

When I just started off, I set a goal: "I need to just say that". I didn't aim as high as I need to be convincing and strong in my voice, I just aimed to actually vocalize it.

Hold to your position and repeat when necessary

This assertiveness technique allows you to feel comfortable by ignoring manipulative verbal side traps, argumentative baiting, and irrelevant logic while sticking to your point. Use calm repetition, say what you want, and stay focused on the issue. You'll find that there is no need to 'hype yourself up' to deal with others.

Example:

- I would like to show you some of our services.

- **No thank you,** I'm not interested.

- I think it can be really interesting for you, it will reduce your costs and increase productivity.

- That may be true, but **I'm not interested** at the moment.

- I understand, you're very busy. Is there anyone else I can talk to?

- **I'm not interested** in the services you're offering, thank you.

- Can I send you an email, so you can give it a thought?

- **Yes.**

- Thank you.

- You're welcome.

You see what has happened here? You're just **repeating** the same phrase adjusting it slightly. You hold on to your position without spending energy explaining why it is so.

Be mindful of your body language

Proper communication involves speech, body language, and listening to the other party. I started incorporating it with focusing on three major elements:

a) Keep an upright posture. What I mean is: Stand straight and tall with your shoulders pulled backward. It is the first thing that projects confidence, you will even feel more confident when you stand straight.

b)   Make eye contact. Maintaining eye contact is an easy way to let the other person know you're engaged and care about what they are saying. It projects confidence and trust. During negotiations, sales people look each other in the eyes and never look down. When they put their demands on the table, they would look straight into your eyes, never down. Otherwise, you will not even take them seriously and will not trust their words. Eye contact seems small but powerful. It's hard to maintain, especially when you're putting together your requests. With practice it gets easier.

c)   Maintain a neutral or positive facial expression. Practicing assertive body language in front of a mirror or with a friend helps to achieve it.

Our body tells more about us than we wish. What I did was I subscribed to a public speaking course to practice on a weekly basis. I have a mentor there who is aware of my goals (one of them is to improve my body language) and points out areas of improvements.

www.ingramcontent.com/pod-product-compliance
Lightning Source LLC
Chambersburg PA
CBHW052137110526
44591CB00012B/1753